Treat You

Treat Your Child's Ear Infections Yourself

Nyema Hermiston
RN ND Adv Dip Hom

Editor: Jon Gamble BA ND Adv Dip Hom
Karuna Publishing
2021

First published in Australia in 2021 by: Karuna Publishing
21 Hambridge Road
Yerrinbool NSW 2575
Australia
ISBN: 978-0-6484144-3-8

All correspondence to to: nyema@karunahealthcare.com.au

Every effort has been made to ensure that this book is free from errors or omissions. However, the author and publishers shall not accept responsibility for injury, loss or damage occasioned to any person acting or refraining from action as a result of material in this book, whether or not such injury, loss or damage is in any way due to any negligent act or omission, breach of duty or default on the part of the author or publishers.

This book is not intended to replace competent medical advice, nor is self-diagnosis recommended in the absence of adequate evaluation by a health professional. In all cases, please seek the advice of a medical professional, and advise him or her of any treatment you are undergoing. The author is a health professional in private practice. The therapeutic recommendations in this book are provided only as examples of successful treatments that have been used with patients. The suggestions in this book are not suitable for patients with severe allergies that cause anaphylactic reactions.

Other Karuna Publishing titles by the same author:
• Treat Your Child Yourself 3rd Edition 2019 Co-written with Jon Gamble
• Good News For People With Bad News First published 2014

www.karunapublishing.com.au

CONTENTS

INTRODUCTION

As a parent, you are your child's best doctor, because it is you who has the opportunity to observe your child closely and are the most familiar with your child's 'normal'.

However, over the last few decades, parents' confidence to treat their children at home for ailments like ear infections before seeking medical care, has been eroded, for fear that they are not qualified or experienced enough to deal with them. Yet it is parents who are in the unique position to observe their child closely and recognise the changes in their condition. I have learned never to doubt a parent's intuition and the ability of a discerning parent to competently care for their own child.

When parents are looking for natural ways to treat their child's ear infections, it is not always easy to know where to find reliable information. Ear infections do need to be treated, but if not antibiotics and painkillers, what will help? This book includes three decades of experience in treating children with drug-free therapies, bringing knowledge for parents back into the home.

Medical treatment for ear problems often means medicating the complaint: acetaminophen (paracetamol/Tylenol) for the fever, antibiotics for the infection and nasal spray for sneezing. While this approach manages the symptoms, it does not always address underlying causes.

Parents generally seek natural treatments because:

- Their child does not tolerate medication well
- Medication is proving ineffective (eg several courses of antibiotics to treat one infection)
- Medications can have unwanted side effects

They want to find underlying causes of their child's complaint. The treatments offered here are simple, sometimes old-fashioned, based on knowledge gained in practice, our colleagues' contributions and not least of all, parents' wisdom and experience.

Along with practical advice, practical applications and nutritional guidelines, homeopathic medicines are a key component of the treatments. It is of course necessary at times for a child to receive medical attention, which is indicated in some sections.

I hope that the treatments offered here help you to gain the confidence that your parents and grandparents once had in treating their families, and to provide you with drug-free solutions for your children, who will in turn treat their own children in the next generation.

Nyema Hermiston

PART ONE

EAR INFECTIONS OVERVIEW

Ear infections in children are common — one might even say normal. They are the most common reason why young children are prescribed antibiotics and painkillers, both of which can impact a child's overall health.

When ear infections become more than an occasional event, leading to a prolonged period of antibiotic prescriptions, it is time to investigate possible reasons why they are susceptible to infection.

Here, you can learn more about the possible reasons why your child may be prone to ear infections, and what you can do for them. Oftentimes, relatively simple interventions make a big difference to the frequency and severity of ear infections.

A big concern for parents when their children get frequent ear infections, is the potential impact they can have on their child's hearing, and therefore their ability to develop their speech. Another is the impact the effects of ear infections have on a child's behaviour. This of course makes it a top priority for parents to promptly treat ear infections to avoid unwanted long-term complications.

As you read on, you will learn about the stages of ear infections and simple treatments you can use when symptoms first appear. You will also learn what you can do to prevent ear infections occurring in the first place. Once you understand why your child is getting ear infections, then it is possible to treat specific aspects of your child's health, resulting in a healthier, happier child.

WHY IS MY CHILD GETTING SO MANY EAR INFECTIONS?

Understanding why ear infections occur helps parents to provide treatment specific to the cause.

*Common **triggers** for ear infections are :*
* Bottle feeding while lying down flat
* Cold or runny nose
* Exposure to cold wind
* Sore throat or tonsillitis
* Teething
* Winter swimming lessons.

BOTTLE FEEDING WHILE LYING FLAT

If you swallow right now, you will hear a 'click'. This means that the tiny, extremely fine tube (eustachian tube) that connects the back of your throat and your middle ear is opening when you swallow and allowing air into your middle ear, the area that gets infected in children. This process maintains a normal pressure level in the middle ear. If a child is drinking while lying down, milk can track up this tube and cause inflammation and blockage. When the eustachian tube becomes blocked, pressure changes in the middle ear cause pain. If it is not alleviated, infection can result.

Elevating the child's head with a pillow or raising the head of their bed while feeding, avoids this problem.

COLD AND RUNNY NOSE

A runny nose leading to a cold is the most common event leading to ear infection. Promptly treating the cold can prove effective. That is not to say the child's cold won't develop, but treatment can make the symptoms shorter-lived and avoid an ear infection developing.

Practical Measures

• Steam from a warm bath, shower or inhalation helps a blocked nose.

- Encourage your child to frequently blow their nose, to keep their ears unblocked.
- Eucalyptus oil helps to clear a blocked nose and make breathing easier.

Nutrition

- A drink of crushed garlic, lemon juice and honey in hot water several times daily. Add freshly grated ginger for a spicy taste.
- Freshly squeezed carrot and/or orange juice provides vitamins A and C.
- Chicken soup made from bone broth is well known for its immune boosting effects.

Supplements

- *Echinacea*, zinc and vitamins C have specific anti-viral effects.
- Vitamin D helps with immune function.

These are easily available over the counter supplements. Take the recommended doses on the label.

Homeopathic Medicines

Pharmacies and health food stores sell homeopathic formulas.

- The tissue salts[1] *Kali Mur* and *Ferrum Phos*, given in the early stages of a cold while the runny nose is still

---

[1] See **Appendix A** - Tissue Salts

clear, can reduce symptoms and the likelihood of an ear infection from developing. Give one dose of each every 1-2 hours for 2 days, then reduce to 2-3 times daily for the next few days until the runny nose has completely stopped.

- If there is sneezing as well, add *Nat Mur* tissue salt. A 'colds and flu' combination remedy with these three tissue salts is available in some brands.

If the nasal discharge becomes coloured, stop the tissue salts and consider one of the medicines below, 2-3 times daily:

- Irritating nasal discharge (skin around the nose becomes red and sore) with watery eyes and sore throat: *Allium Cepa 30c.*
- Thick, creamy/yellow discharge and blocked ears, in a child prone to ear infections, *Pulsatilla 30c.*
- Blocked nose at night, with thick nasal mucus, *Ammonium Carb 30c.*
- When the cold moves quickly to the chest: *Phosphorus 30c.*
- For an established cold with a thick yellow nasal discharge, *Lycopodium 30c.*

EXPOSURE TO COLD WIND

Some children are prone to earaches after they have been out in the cold, especially if it is windy as well. This may set up an ear inflammation and cause pain, which may be severe. In the first 24-48 hours, this will be ear *pain* and not an established ear infection. The outer ear may be quite red.

When cold air is the clear cause of the earache, the homeopathic medicine *Aconite*, given within the first 12 hours after exposure to the cold, can reduce the inflammation and therefore the pain. The trick is to give this medicine as soon as the ear pain starts, every ½ - 1 hourly until the pain settles. Redose if the pain returns.

A headband covering the ears underneath a beanie in cold conditions may prevent ear pain from developing.

SORE THROAT OR TONSILLITIS

Some children develop a sore throat before an ear infection develops. Normal tonsil colour is the same pink as the rest of the mouth. If the tonsils are red, this is the likely cause of the sore throat. If you can see one or both tonsils bulging towards the uvula, then they are enlarged. Sometimes the glands in the neck are swollen. Treating the *very first symptoms* can stop tonsillitis from progressing. If there are white spots on the tonsils, sharp pain and difficulty swallowing, with a fever over 38.5ºC, seek professional care.

Practical Measures

- Rest in the early stages of tonsillitis for a faster recovery.
- A lemon juice and honey drink with garlic, is a good antibiotic drink.
- Another antibiotic drink is to boil one onion in a cup of water. Remove the onion, add honey and slowly sip.

Supplements

- Vitamin C lozenges
- Garlic
- *Echinace*a.

Homeopathic Medicines

- At the first sign of any sore throat, use *Ferrum Phos 30c* every one to two hours. If you only have the *Ferrum Phos* tissue salt2, use it hourly for 1-2 days.
- For sore throat, swollen glands and fever below 38.5ºC, give *Hepar Sulph 30c* every 1-2 hours, gradually reducing the frequency as symptoms improve.
- Sharp pain felt in the ear or head when the child swallows, and *Hepar Sulph* has not helped, give *Phytolacca* 30c 1-2 hourly.
- If the sore throat has come on suddenly, the child is weak, and there are no swollen glands, use *Phosphorus 30c* twice daily.

---

² See **Appendix A** - Tissue Salts

TEETHING

Some children become prone to ear infections when they are teething. Despite a body of medical opinion insisting that teething does not cause symptoms in children, we see many babies and toddlers affected by symptoms during teething.

Many children have been helped through teething with homeopathic medicines, which can help to prevent ear an infection from developing.

Homeopathic Medicines

Pharmacies and health food stores sell homeopathic formulas for teething.

- *Chamomilla 30c* is well known for its ability to settle teething pain, especially in a child who is irritable and unpleasable, wanting to be picked up and then not. Give 5 drops every 5-10 minutes, until the child settles.
- When all the teeth seem to be coming through at once, giving *Chamomilla 30c* two or three times a day routinely, until the teething period is over, helps to manage the pain.
- When a child is fine during the day, but wakeful at night, give one dose of *Coffea 30c* at bedtime, and repeat on waking in the night.
- For severe teething pain, when *Chamomilla* hasn't helped, give *Kreosotum 30c* twice daily.

WINTER SWIMMING LESSONS

Some children do not tolerate swimming lessons in cold weather, and catch colds easily which may lead to ear infections. Parents can be reassured that there is enough time during summer for children to learn to swim, so avoiding this common trigger is possible.

If winter swimming is unavoidable, taking supplements like zinc, vitamin C and Cod Liver Oil, which contains vitamins A & D, may help to build resistance to developing colds.

COMMON UNDERLYING CAUSES OF EAR INFECTIONS

Underlying causes for ear infections are:

- Food sensitivities
- Enlarged adenoids
- Poor resistance to viruses and gut dysbiosis
- Nutritional deficiency: **see Appendices B i) & B ii).**

FOOD SENSITIVITIES

Some of the many symptoms that point towards food sensitivities:

- Abdominal pain and bloating

- Behavioural issues
- Concentration & learning difficulty
- Constipation and/or diarrhoea
- **Frequent infections — colds, ear infections, tonsillitis**
- Hyperactivity
- Skin problems
- Sleep problems.

Tackling food sensitivities is best done with the help of a health professional, but these suggestions may help to begin with. It can be really worthwhile (and surprising) to keep a diet diary for a few weeks, noting the timing of problematic symptoms and behaviour.

Practical measures

- Try a simple diet so you can see which foods affect your child. Common problem foods are eggs, dairy products, wheat, corn, nuts, soya beans and food additives. Remove all these foods from the diet. After 3 - 4 weeks, reintroducing the foods, one by one will reveal problem foods, as your child will have obvious symptoms, such as skin reactions, tummy pain, runny nose, and behaviour changes.
- Using organic, unprocessed (foods that have not been pre packaged and prepared) foods saves a lot of time checking labels. Additive Guides are available online. Significant improvements are often seen using this measure alone.

- Drink plenty of filtered water.
- Treat gut problems by removing sugars, increasing vegetables and using probiotics. See **Appendix C**: Homemade Probiotics.

Safe foods are generally:

- Meats, chicken and fish
- Pear, golden delicious apple
- Vegetables
- White and brown rice
- Gluten free grains like rice, buckwheat, quinoa and millet
- Coconut cream, coconut milk and coconut oil.

Supplements

- Cod Liver oil
- Fish oil
- Probiotics
- Zinc.

If none of the above help, see a health professional for testing and diagnosis. For information about food sensitivity and allergy testing, **see Appendix D.**

ENLARGED ADENOIDS

Signs of enlarged adenoids are mouth breathing, snoring and irregular breathing during sleep (sleep apnoea).

Children with enlarged adenoids speak with a nasal sound, and sound like they have a blocked nose much of the time. They may tilt their head back to make it easier to breathe through their mouth, especially at night. Enlarged tonsils often accompany large adenoids, which can predispose to tonsillitis and be a trigger for frequent ear infections.

Symptoms:

- Grumpy on waking
- Daytime fatigue
- Hyperactivity
- Poor concentration
- Poor mood control.

The medical treatment for problematic enlarged adenoids is surgical removal. In some children, this may ultimately be necessary. First though, some simple strategies to reduce the size of adenoids (and tonsils) can help to avoid surgery. Once breathing is improved, children become happier, have better concentration, wake in a better mood and have improved stamina.

Practical Measures

- Identify food sensitivities and eliminate them from the diet *for at least one month*. The most common foods that cause lymphatic congestion of adenoids are dairy, wheat, eggs and soy products. If it is not clear by that stage which foods are affecting your child, when you reintroduce the foods one by one, symptoms alert you to the problem foods. Your health professional can order an IgG food panel test to identify food sensitivities, which is a faster way of finding out which food or foods your child is sensitive to.

- The *Buteyko Method*[3] uses nose-breathing exercises. If your child has asthma as well as enlarged adenoids, *Buteyko* breathing exercises can significantly help both problems.

Homeopathic Medicine

Many children have been spared removal of their adenoids and tonsils using homeopathic medicines. For an individualised prescription see a qualified homeopath.

---

[3] *Buteyko* Method www.buteyko.com is a drug free method for managing asthma and other breathing problems.

POOR RESISTANCE TO VIRUSES AND GUT DYSBIOSIS

See **Appendices E and F**

When, despite the best of care, your child picks up infections easily and repeatedly, their immune system may be under functioning. This can be for many reasons. A common one is having had antibiotics and/or paracetamol in their first year of life, which can affect normal development of gut flora. It is possible to restore gut function, and therefore immune function, over time. If your child needs antibiotics on a regular basis and you are not comfortable about it, seek professional help to find different ways of treating your child when needed.

Lifestyle changes:

First steps are to remove processed and sugary foods from the diet and introduce regular protein meals, fresh fruit, vegetables and whole grains. Easier said than done, and this requires time and determination. Avoiding snacks between meals is a good starting point, because it means your child will be hungry at meal times and more likely to eat the healthy food you provide for them. Offer non-sugary drinks or a piece of fruit between meals if needed.

If your child is craving foods such as milk or bread, this may indicate that these foods are problematic. Cravings can cause real conflict in the kitchen. One hard line strategy is not to have problem foods in the house. Take your child shopping and get them to choose alternatives. There are many support groups for parents around developing healthier eating habits for their children.

Plenty of sun exposure, filtered water, and a good quality multivitamin and mineral supplement daily helps to build up general health.

To encourage healthy gut function, you can make your own low cost probiotics. **See Appendix C.**

NUTRITIONAL DEFICIENCY

See **Appendix B** for food /nutrient lists.

It may come as a surprise that your child could be low in some nutrients. Boosting the levels of specific nutrients can be helpful in avoiding the uptake of community-spread bugs and the resulting runny noses, colds and ear infections.

1. The first nutrient is **iron**. Iron deficiency is surprisingly common in children under two years old, especially if they don't like eating meat. You can tell if your child needs more iron by checking the colour of their inner lower eyelid. It should look tomato red. Children with low iron may lack stamina and need more sleep than other children. Iron deficiency alone is enough to affect immune response and is easily remedied by taking an iron supplement, available from pharmacies. Spaghetti bolognese is an excellent way of providing red meat and hiding lots of vegetables in the sauce. The trick is to make sure they eat all of the sauce and not just the pasta. If needed, serve the sauce first, then the pasta.

2. The second nutrient is **zinc** — an essential element for normal immune function. Deficiency can show as white spots on the fingernails, in some, but not all children who are low in zinc. It can be difficult to get

enough zinc from the diet in countries where the zinc levels in the soil are low. Again, a supplement is the easiest way of providing zinc to your child.

3. In the days where children tend to spend more time indoors than out, **vitamin D** deficiency is also possible. As well as ensuring healthy bones, vitamin D plays a significant role in immune function, and may even help to reduce allergic symptoms. Plenty of sun exposure without sunscreen is important — at least one hour daily in winter time. Cod Liver Oil is an old-fashioned supplement that provides vitamins A and D. Chewable capsules that children like are available.

4. **Magnesium** has many benefits, not least of all enabling the absorption of other minerals — including **vitamin D**. Signs your child may be low in magnesium are leg cramps, headaches, irritability, hyperactivity, restless sleep and unexplained nervousness. The body uses up magnesium during stress, so it is important there are good levels of this mineral. Magnesium can be taken orally, via a daily Epsom Salts bath, or as a skin cream.

PART TWO

STAGES OF EAR INFECTIONS

EAR PAIN

Infection is not always the cause of ear pain. When the eustachian tube (that connects the middle ear to the back of the nose) blocks, it results in pressure changes in the middle ear. You can hear the 'click' of the eustachian tube opening and closing when you swallow. When this function is temporarily lost, pain can result. Treating ear pain promptly can minimise symptoms and avoid it progressing to an infection.

Practical Measures

- Jaw movement helps eustachian tube function, so if your child is old enough, ask them to yawn, chew gum or swallow while pinching their nose.
- A heat pack applied directly to the ear.

Homeopathic Medicines

Give every 15-30 minutes, reducing the frequency with improvement:

- For earache without infection – *Kali Mur 6x* tissue salt [4].
- At the very first sign of a cold, give *Ferrum Phos 6x* and *Kali Mur* tissue salts every few hours for a few days.
- When ear pain strikes suddenly after being out in the cold, with no other symptoms other than a red ear, *Aconite 30c.*
- The external ear is bright red, with throbbing pain, *Belladonna 3c.*
- Ear pain during teething, *Chamomilla 30c.*
- A combination remedy of *Aconite 30c, Belladonna 30c* and *Chamomilla 30c,* or '**ABC**' is a broad spectrum treatment.

---

[4] See **Appendix A** – Tissue Salts

ONGOING EAR PAIN

Practical Measures

Try one of these home remedies to put into the ear, *provided there is no drum rupture.* You can tell if there is a drum rupture due to a visible discharge around the ear or on the pillow.

- A few drops of hydrogen peroxide.
- A few drops of warmed coconut oil.
- Mullein ear drops
- Sleep with the head above the body, by raising the bed head, or use an extra pillow.
- Drinking and chewing can unblock ear and help with pain.
- An onion poultice is a popular home remedy. Raw onion wrapped in cotton gauze applied to the ear can ease pain. Recipes for this are online.
- A few drops of onion and/or garlic juice may be more effective.

Homeopathic Medicines - give every 15 minutes until pain settles

- Pain comes on suddenly, after being in cold wind: *Aconite 30c*
- The external ear is bright red and feels hot to touch, *Belladonna 3c*

- Irritable during teething along with ear pain give *Chamomilla 30c*
- ABC: *Combining Aconite 30c, Belladonna 30c and Chamomilla 30c* is convenient. Mix a few drops or pillules in a glass of water and sip frequently.

For less distressing ear pain

- If the nose discharge has become yellow/green, ears are blocked and hearing is affected, give *Pulsatilla 30c* three times daily until nasal mucus clears.
- A clingy, miserable child, with reduced hearing, *Pulsatilla 30c* every one or two hours, reducing on improvement.
- Ear pain that occurs only at night not due to teething – *Mercurius Sol 30c* every hour while awake, starting with a dose at bedtime.
- If there is a sore throat with swollen glands, *Hepar Sulph 30c* every four hours until pain has been absent for 24 hours. Reduce to twice daily for another few days.

EARDRUM RUPTURE

When an ear drum ruptures during a middle ear infection, nature is doing its work of ridding the middle ear of infected material. It results in sudden relief of pain and rapid resolution of the infection. Some ruptures are preceded by severe pain and screaming, others 'pop' with little distress to the child. In young children, eardrums heal quickly. Provided ruptures do not occur too often, there is no damage to hearing. No immediate treatment is needed once the eardrum has ruptured. Some children are prescribed antibiotics after an eardrum rupture, but this is not necessary unless ear discomfort continues. The best treatment now, is to prevent further ear infections by addressing underlying causes, like poor immunity, tonsil/adenoid problems, and food sensitivity.

NB: *If pain continues **after** an eardrum rupture, seek prompt medical attention.*

To heal the eardrum after a rupture

Give these medicines 3 times daily:

*   To aid healing and reduce the discharge, give *Kali Sulph 6x* 5 tissue salt three times daily for one week.
*   *Silica 6x* twice daily to heal the eardrum

---

[5] See **Appendix A**

!! Avoid any liquid getting in to the ear if the drum has ruptured.

HEARING PROBLEMS

Poor hearing in children is most commonly caused by fluid in the middle ear, which may be the result of having had one or more ear infections. When the fluid has been present for 3 months, it develops into 'glue ear'.

Children can adapt to having poor hearing very well, which means parents may not notice any problem to begin with. Children learn to read facial cues and even lip-read. You can see this by the absolute concentration on a child's face when you are speaking to them. This could be why they don't respond to your voice when they are not looking at you directly. They may not be ignoring you. A hearing problem like this can go undetected until it becomes really obvious — usually at around four years old.

Check your child's hearing

Parents can easily check if their child's lack of response is 'selective hearing' or not. In a quiet room, ask your child to stand with their back to you 4-5 metres away and whisper something to them. Then ask him or her to repeat it. A child with normal hearing can hear a very quiet whisper and repeat it back to you perfectly. Confusion with the words means that their hearing is affected. Repeat this test a few times when they don't have a cold or blocked nose. If hearing is consistently poor, have an audiology test done.

Poor hearing can affect behaviour

Even when a child compensates well to undetected hearing loss, they miss out on hearing conversations, and feel left out of games and activities and will display signs of frustration.

Practical Measures

- Have a hearing test with an audiologist
- For blocked eustachian tube, use an '*Otovent*'6
- Have adenoids checked. Symptoms of enlarged adenoids are noisy breathing, consistent mouth breathing and snoring.

GLUE EAR

Glue ear can develop with or without repeated ear infections. When fluid has been present in the middle ear for more than three months, it thickens and is then classified as 'glue ear'. This is diagnosed by a

---

6 *Otovent* is a nose-balloon for children to blow into, which equalises ear pressure by unblocking the eustachian tube and improves hearing. See Appendix H

tympanogram[7]. By the time glue ear is detected, it is usually well established and can be obstinate to treat. Treatment centres on unblocking the eustachian tubes and treating the underlying causes, such as enlarged adenoids, food sensitivities, environmental allergies and poor immunity. Glue ear can affect hearing, which is the main concern. Ear tubes called grommets can be surgically inserted to treat glue ear, but there is some debate about this intervention offering long-term benefit compared to conservative treatment.

Practical Measures

- Unblocking the eustachian tube is key to reducing middle ear fluid.
- Children 3½ years and older are able blow up medical grade balloons called *Otovents* using their nose, which can rapidly clear the eustachian tubes. See **Appendix G.**
- Have an audiology test every three months to monitor progress.
- See your health professional to assess causes, such as food sensitivity.

---

[7] A Tympanogram is a test conducted by an audiologist that measures middle ear pressure and eardrum vibration to assess hearing and identify hearing loss.

Homeopathic Medicines

- *Pulsatilla 30c* plus *Kali Mur 6x* tissue salt[8] given twice daily long-term can improve hearing.
- If there is no improvement after one month, see your health professional.

OTHER SYMPTOMS

Behaviour problems

Children who can't hear properly can get easily frustrated, so poor hearing could underly behavioural issues. A home hearing test (see above) can help parents recognise the possibility of reduced hearing.

Crying Babies

In a baby who normally settles well, and does not suffer from colic or reflux, the only sign of an ear infection may be that they cry after being put down to sleep. This is more likely if the baby has a cold or is teething.

Poor Balance

Ongoing ear infections can affect balance. Have an ear check before looking for underlying problems.

---

[8] See **Appendix A** – Tissue Salts

Earwax

Earwax is normal and some children produce more than others. Only when the earwax solidifies and a waxy 'plug' develops, affecting hearing, it becomes problematic. Otherwise, the presence of earwax doesn't need treatment.

Practical Measures

- A few drops of olive or almond oil, glycerine, or food grade hydrogen peroxide in one ear for five nights, with the child lying on one side so that the oil stays inside the ear. Treat one ear for one week, then the other ear for another week. Once softened, ask your doctor to syringe the ear(s) to remove the softened wax.
- Wax softening products are available from pharmacies. Lying in the bath with ears submerged adds to the softening effect.

NB: Don't try to remove earwax with cotton buds, as this pushes the wax further inside the ear, and can worsen the problem.

Fever

Babies and toddlers can't tell you how they are feeling, so they show you with their symptoms. If there is a fever with ear tugging and otherwise unexplained crying, suspect an earache or infection.

Fever is a symptom of infection and *not an illness in itself.* It can be reassuring to know that a fever is doing the job it is supposed to do, even with an ear infection. It is a healthy immune response and the body's way of extinguishing the organism that is causing the infection.

In our experience, attempting to reduce the fever with medication is likely to ***prolong*** the fever. Some medical authorities recommend avoiding reducing fevers and find that the fever reduces more quickly without medication.

While a temperature of over 38°C is considered to be a fever, some children with a 39°C fever have little more than a red face. He/she is tolerating fever well, so there is little need for concern. Other children look very unwell with a lower temperature. ***Let the state of your child be your guide, rather than the number on the thermometer.***

*** Having said that, once a fever reaches 40°C, it is time to seek medical help.

Parents are understandably fearful a fever could cause a febrile convulsion; however, these are uncommon. Febrile convulsions usually occur as the fever rapidly rises. By the time the fever has peaked, the risk period of having a febrile convulsion is usually over.

Practical Measures

• Check temperature hourly.

- Identify a likely cause of the fever by checking which illnesses are circulating in your community.
- See if you can detect ear inflammation or pain.
- Give plenty of fluids, but little food.
- Light clothing only.
- It is not necessary to cool your child down other than for comfort.

Homeopathic Medicines

To contain fever (not necessarily bring it down), give one of these medicines *half-hourly until improvement:*

- For fever under 38.5°C, give *Ferrum Phos 30c. Ferrum Phos* tissue salt [9] will also help.
- Sudden fever after being out in cold wind: *Aconite 30c.*
- Fever over 38.5°C with bright red face, dazed and lethargic: *Belladonna 30c.*
- The child is weak, lethargic, flushed and drowsy, and refuses drinks – *Gelsemium 6c or 30c.*
- Fever at around midnight, the child is anxious and restless: *Arsenicum 30c.*

Cautions:

Seek medical help if one or more of these symptoms are present

- High pitched weak, continuous cry
- Floppy, unresponsive and disoriented (no eye contact)

----

[9] See **Appendix A** – Tissue Salts

- Ongoing irritability
- Repeated green vomiting
- Repeated diarrhoea
- Unable to keep fluids down
- Bulging or sunken fontanelle in babies
- Stiff neck
- Skin colour pale, blue or ashen
- Difficulty breathing — stomach sucking under the ribs
- Grunting, fast breathing
- Pain in abdomen, chest or head
- Purplish pinprick rash that doesn't fade when pressed with a glass.
- *Signs of dehydration:* sunken eyes, dark coloured, strong smelling urine — no urination for eight hours, or much less than usual. The younger the child, the greater the risk of dehydration.

If you are concerned about your child during any fever, seek medical attention.

PART THREE

MEDICATIONS

- Penicillin
- Paracetamol - It's Safe, Isn't It?
- Getting Off The Antibiotic Treadmill

PENICILLIN

When penicillin was introduced in the 1940s, it was used as a life-saving treatment for serious bacterial infections. Some 80 years later, antibiotics are used for ailments that are capable of resolving themselves.

The World Health Organisation recommends antibiotic prescriptions be made after *isolating the bacteria before giving an antibiotic.* This means taking an ear, nose or throat swab before prescribing an antibiotics. In reality, this doesn't usually happen, as it means waiting for 1-2 days for an antibiotic prescription. These days, few people would accept that.

There are inherent problems with frequent antibiotic use, particularly in children under one year old. Research is showing that children who are given antibiotics in the first year of life are more likely to develop asthma in their later years.

The increasing use of antibiotics in children from 1977 to the early 1990s led to what federal health officials called "a public health crisis in antibiotic resistance". The Henry Ford study [10] followed 448 children from birth to seven years. The study found that by age 7, children given at least one antibiotic in the first six months of their life were 1.5 times more likely to develop allergies than those who had not received antibiotics. The study also found a link between antibiotics, allergies and asthma in children. The study's authors recommended more prudence in prescribing antibiotics to young children.

---

[10] https://www.sciencedaily.com/releases/2003/10/031001064200.htm last accessed 15th July 2020

Also, Christine Cole Johnson, PhD, the study's lead author, suggested that use of antibiotics may affect the gastrointestinal tract and alter the development of a child's immune system.

The problem of antibiotic overuse was debated in British parliament in 1998 and a strategy to reduce antibiotic use was developed.[11]

Antibiotics should be used "prudently and appropriately" to "prevent, delay, and control" increasing resistance. Up to 75% of antibiotic use is of "questionable therapeutic value." Some patients regard antibiotics as a "rapid route back to school or work" — "doctors could only cope with a certain amount of distress before they collude."

Recommendations:

No antibiotics for:

- Simple coughs and colds
- Viral sore throats
- Uncomplicated cystitis
- Acne
- All prophylactic (just in case) prescriptions eg dental, wounds, labour.

---

[11] https://www.ncbi.nlm.nih.gov/pmc/articles/PMC1113840/ last accessed 15th July 2020

Negative effects of Antibiotics:

- Diarrhoea – destroyed gut flora
- Link with asthma and allergies
- Compromised immunity
- Early use in babies with allergic mothers leading to an increased incidence in allergies.

PARACETAMOL - IT'S SAFE, ISN'T IT?

Once the risks of gastric bleeding from taking aspirin were recognised, paracetamol became the go-to alternative. Paracetamol was found to help reduce fever in the 1940s, followed by the recognition of it also being a painkiller. The developed world has used paracetamol for the past 70 years, believing that it is safe for babies and young children. It has become commonplace for children between one and three years old to be given paracetamol. If we were to look for an explanation why so many young children suffer from allergies, a growing number of studies linking allergies with paracetamol helps to shed light on this question.

A study of over 200,000 children from 31 countries, published in the medical journal *The Lancet*[12] suggests that using paracetamol in the first year of life is linked

---

[12] https://www.abc.net.au/science/articles/2008/09/19/2369275.htm

to an increased risk of asthma and other allergies. *Giving paracetamol to treat fever in children in the first year of life means that a child has a 46% greater risk of having asthma symptoms at age 6 to 7.* The study also found that 6 to 7 year-olds who had taken paracetamol once a month in the 12 months prior had a had a *three fold increase risk of asthma.* The study acknowledges that it is common knowledge among scientists that paracetamol reduces antioxidant defences, and switches the immune system to become more reactive.

Another study[13] showed that exposure to paracetamol can suppress immune function that could have an impact on resistance to infection.

Parents have been educated to treat fevers. With more understanding, parents can recognise that a short-lived high fever in a child is a healthy response to an infection. Sometimes a fever comes and goes within 24 hours and the cause is never known. Such fevers are known to be a feature of a childhood development which strengthens of the immune system.

If there is a family history of allergies, avoiding paracetamol in the first year of life becomes even more

---

[13] Effects of Prophylactic and Therapeutic Paracetamol Treatment during Vaccination on Hepatitis B Antibody Levels https://journals.plos.org/plosone/article?id=10.1371/journal.pone.0098175 last accessed 23rd July 2020

important. This does leave parents up in the air about what to do when their child has fever and/or pain. The role of other methods of treatment comes into play here, and offers parents more options. The therapies we offer here, are nutrition, trusted practical interventions and homeopathic medicines.

GETTING OFF THE ANTIBIOTIC TREADMILL

Children who have chronic ear infections can become caught in a vicious cycle of needing an antibiotic prescription every five or six weeks, or ongoing low-dose antibiotics for several months. This comes at a price, due to the negative impact on beneficial gut bacteria and therefore immune function, or 'resistance to infection'.

Natural medicine practitioners do not have access to antibiotics. Instead, we use natural medicines that are capable of adequately dealing with infections, including ear infections. Once parents see how well children respond to natural medicines for ear nose and throat infections, they develop confidence that their child will recover well without needing to take antibiotics.

It takes 24 - 48 hours for antibiotics to have an effect on ear pain. For this reason, more doctors are adopting a 'watch and wait' approach for 48 hours, offering pain relief as needed, to see if the infection settles without treatment. Studies show that without antibiotic therapy, 70 per cent of children recover from acute ear infections within 2-3 days and 80 per cent recover within 10 days[14] and emphasise the benefits of 'watchful waiting'.

Even so, many children who suffer ear infections, are prescribed one or more courses of antibiotics to treat a single ear infection. When a child is in a cycle of repeatedly needing antibiotics just weeks after their previous ear infection, this is known as 'the antibiotic treadmill'.

While no one can question the need for antibiotics for some infections, needing repeated courses of antibiotics for chronic ear infections indicates that the treatment is not addressing the problem.

For sleep-deprived parents, the thought of not taking another course of antibiotics for the ear infection which is keeping them awake at night can be daunting; what to do next time your child has a high fever, is crying with pain, needing more time off school or away from day care and your sick leave at work is running out? In this situation, parents who have decided to try a different treatment path for their child, will generally need support to manage the next infection, which will surely come. There is a lot that can be done in between ear infections to improve a child's

---

[14] New AOM treatment guidelines emphasise watchful waiting https://www.clinicaladvisor.com/home/web-exclusives/new-aom-treatment-guidelines-emphasize-watchful-waiting/ last accessed 23rd July 2020

resistance to infection, through improved nutrition, and gut health to enhance immune function, so the first thing to do is provide treatment as soon as they have recovered from the latest ear infection.

When we treat children who have been unwell for many months or longer and have a long history of antibiotic use, it can be stressful for parents to step off this treadmill. Sometimes, a high fever is 'the fever you have to have' in order to get better from the cycle of illness and medication. It is possible though, and well worth the effort to learn how to strengthen your child's general health, so that they suffer fewer infections and tolerate them better when they do.

A common perception is that natural medicines work more slowly than medical drugs. This can be true of nutritional therapy and gut restoration, but the correctly prescribed homeopathic medicine can quickly relieve pain and reduce fever in a distressed child. This has been verified in clinical trials.[15] Once parents have experienced the effect of a correctly prescribed homeopathic remedy in their child, they feel more confident in dealing with future infections. Ideally, taking the step off the antibiotic treadmill is done with the help of a health professional.

---

[15] Acute otitis media in children. Comparison between conventional and homeopathic therapy Int J Clin Pharmacol Ther 1997 Jul; 35(7):296-301. *https://pubmed.ncbi.nlm.nih.gov/9247843/* last accessed 23rd July 2020

Getting your child back to normal health is rewarding when it results in a child with more energy and better mood. Along the way, parents learn the strategies to deal with the next runny nose, and learn to recognise and treat early symptoms. I hope that you find the information provided in this book helpful.

APPENDICES

APPENDIX A
TISSUE SALTS

Biochemical tissue salts, or 'Schuessler Salts' are over-the-counter minerals ideal for home use, to treat a range of ailments. Children like chewing them and they are safe for pregnant women. Tablets are usually given two to four times daily.

Tissue salts are based on the principle that when one or more of the twelve minerals present in the tissues necessary for cell function are lacking, symptoms develop. Treatment delivers mineral salts back to the body in an easily assimilated form; micro-doses that pass rapidly into the blood stream.

NAME	COMPOSITION	INDICATIONS
CALC FLUOR	Calcium Fluoride	Strengthens tooth enamel, nails.
CALC PHOS	Calcium Phosphate	Poor absorption of food. Aids digestion. Promotes strong teeth & bones.
CALC SULPH	Calcium Sulphate	Skin remedy, when pus is present.

NAME	COMPOSITION	INDICATIONS
FERRUM PHOS	Iron Phosphate	For fevers & first stage of colds. Anti-inflammatory for the first stage of any illness.
KALI MUR	Potassium Chloride	Any illness with white mucus — eg second stage of a cold.
KALI PHOS	Potassium Phosphate	Nerve nutrient. For hard to settle, nervous children.
KALI SULPH	Potassium Sulphate	Yellow/green discharges from nose or ear. Dry flaky skin.
MAG PHOS	Magnesium Phosphate	For cramps, spasms and tension headaches.
NAT MUR	Sodium Chloride	Watery nasal discharge, sneezing, allergic reactions, like hives.
NAT PHOS	Sodium Phosphate	Poor digestion after excess sugar. Acidity.
NAT SULPH	Sodium Sulphate	Colds and asthma worse in wet or damp weather.

NAME	COMPOSITION	INDICATIONS
SILICA	Silica	Boils, styes, slow wound healing. Brittle nails, fine hair. For delicate, shy children.

Tissue salts can be given in combinations of two or three at one time. There are 21 combinations for specific conditions available from health stores and pharmacies. Tissue Salts handbooks with prescribing guidelines are available at many purchase outlets. Whole Health Now www.wholehealthnow.com/homeopathy_info/weblinks3. html lists international outlets.

APPENDIX B
MINERALS

The importance of adequate minerals in a child's diet cannot be underestimated.

Magnesium, zinc, copper, iodine and iron are often found lacking in children suffering from conditions like allergies, poor immunity, low energy, irritability, hyperactivity and insomnia. Copper is often found in high levels in hyperactive, irritable children. Correcting the imbalance can lead to a significant resolution of the child's health issue.

Mineral levels can be tested via a Hair Tissue Mineral Analysis[16] or *Oligoscan*[17] available from some health professionals.

---

[16] Hair Mineral Analysis assesses long–term mineral absorption via a sample of scalp hair, available from naturopaths and integrative doctors.

[17] Oligoscan is available in many countries. See www.oligoscan.com

Mineral	Deficiency signs & symptoms	Food Sources
Calcium	Irritability, slow to learn, poor immunity.	Dried figs, cheese, parsley, sardines, sesame seeds, cooked spinach, parsnip.
Magnesium	Irritability, hyperactivity, leg cramps, poor sleeping, tics, tremors.	Nuts, dates, figs, whole grain breads (check labels) cocoa powder.
Zinc	Allergies, lowered immunity, poor wound healing. White spots on the nails in some children.	Beef, ginger, sunflower seeds, pumpkin seeds, whole grains.
Iron	Pale (or rosy) cheeks! Poor appetite, fatigue, poor resistance to infection. Child likes to chew paper, cardboard or peculiar things.	Apricots, red meat, parsley, sunflower seeds, pumpkin seeds, whole grains.
Iodine	Physical and mental developmental delay, learning disorders.	Fish and seafood, oysters, eggs, seaweed sushi, miso soup, iodised salt, kelp, eggs.

VITAMINS

A look at the symptoms of B vitamin deficiencies, reveals a number of commonly experienced mental and behavioural symptoms. Picky eaters and children on restricted diets are vulnerable to B vitamin deficiency.

Liquid and chewable supplements for young children are easier to give than tablets and capsules.

Vitamin	Deficiency symptoms	Food Sources
B1	Poor concentration, memory deficits, gut disorders, muscle weakness and slow growth.	Peas, beans, lentils, liver, pork, nuts, wheat germ, whole grains and yeast.
B2	Cracks in the corners of the mouth, cracked and sore lips, hypersensitivity, mapped tongue, and sores in and around the mouth.	Avocados, beans, currants, eggs, dairy products, organ meats, sprouts, whole grains, yeast and broccoli.
B3	Abdominal bloating, low stomach acid, diarrhoea, red inflamed tongue, gut inflammation and scaly dermatitis.	Almonds, peanuts, sunflower seeds, chicken, eggs, peas, beans, lentils, meat, salmon, mackerel and yeast.

Vitamin	Deficiency symptoms	Food Sources
B6	Anaemia, poor appetite, skin rashes, and poor immunity.	Brewer's yeast, oats, chicken, egg yolk, beans, peas, lentils, peanuts, walnuts, salmon, mackerel.
B9 (Folate)	Anaemia, constipation, cracked lips, diarrhoea, forgetfulness, slow growth, hostility, mental sluggishness, short sightedness and neural tube defects that can cause spina bifida.	Beans, lentils, eggs, green leafy vegetables, organ meats, yeast.
B12	Low stomach acid, anaemia, Attention Deficit Disorder (ADD), poor concentration, depression, mood swings, poor appetite, slow growth and temper tantrums.	Salmon, sardines, herring, oysters, egg yolk, kidney, liver, meat, milk. **Healthy gut bacteria:** Raw foods, fermented foods like miso, sauerkraut, kim chi, homemade salsa, kefir yoghurt and good quality plain yoghurt .

Vitamins A, C and D are essential for optimal immune function. Sources are fresh fruit and vegetables, plus Cod Liver Oil and safe sun exposure.

APPENDIX C
HOMEMADE PROBIOTICS

Probiotic foods are equally effective as commercial probiotics and are easily made at home. They are:
- Kefir yoghurt
- Pickles
- Sauerkraut.

KEFIR YOGHURT

Organisms Found In Kefir Yoghurt

The range of organisms found in Kefir yoghurt is wider than any probiotic you can purchase. It contains more than thirty types of lactobacilli, acetobacter, streptococci, lactococci and yeasts.

Once you have your own Kefir grain, you can make your own yoghurt with fresh milk at room temperature, because it regenerates perpetually in fresh milk, at room temperature. Kefir grains do not deteriorate; all that is required is fresh milk of your choice and five minutes of your time each day.

Kefir can be made at any temperature from 4 to 40°C. At lower temperatures it will take longer to set.

As soon as you get your grain, put it in half a cup of cow, goat, soy or coconut milk, cover, and leave on the kitchen bench until it thickens. Kefir yoghurt is runnier than commercial yoghurt. As the grain grows, it will set larger quantities of milk. Eventually the grain will grow so that it sets up to one litre of your preferred milk at a time. The first few batches of Kefir you make may not yield as much yoghurt, or taste as good as later, as the grains are "waking up".

How To Make Kefir Yoghurt

Utensils:

- A 500 ml ceramic or glass container with a cover
- A container to store kefir in the fridge
- A sieve to strain the freshly made Kefir

Use ANY type of milk (including coconut, soy, rice milk, powdered, sheep and goats') **except long life milks.**

Method:

5. Put the Kefir grains in your container, add your preferred milk and cover.

6. Add a dessert spoon of milk powder if you prefer thicker yoghurt.

7. Stir every 12 hours or so. Setting time will vary, from

one to several days, according to the strength of the grain, room temperature and the type of milk.

8.   When set, pour through a sieve, and retain the kefir grain.

9.   Spoon unwashed grains back into the 500 ml jar and repeat the process. Wash utensils in unchlorinated water.

NB. Never heat the milk, as excess temperature is one of the few things that will kill the grains. Similarly, never use bleaches or detergents for cleaning the utensils you use when making Kefir, as these may kill or taint the grain.

Sharing grains:

When the grains are about the size of a walnut, small pieces drop off readily. *A grain the size of 1mm diameter is enough to grow new grains!* Take a small grain and grow it for a week in the same jar, then pass it on when it's bigger.

Storing Grains:

Store in the refrigerator in a jar covered with filtered, unchlorinated water. Refresh the water every week.

USE CLEAN WATER: CHLORINATED TOWN WATER MAY DAMAGE THE GRAINS.

Not Sure How to Start?

To see a simple demonstration: http://www.youtube.com/watch?v=g8inJzX-6yE

References:

- *Encyclopaedia of Food Science & Food Technology & Nutrition* 5 ISBN: 0-12-226855-5, ACADEMIC PRESS-> Food Technology and Nutrition: "Kefir" pp 1804-1808.
- *International Journal of Systematic Bacteriology* 44 (3) 435-439 (1994) [21 ref. En] — * two new organisms recently discovered!

SAUERKRAUT & PICKLES:

Kimchi (Korean Sauerkraut) - Makes one quart (1200mls)

1 head Wombok cabbage (also known as Napa, or Chinese cabbage)

1 bunch spring onions, chopped

1 cup grated carrot

½ cup grated daikon radish (optional)

1 tablespoon of freshly grated ginger

3 cloves of garlic, peeled and minced

½ teaspoon of dried chilli flakes

1 teaspoon of salt

4 tablespoons of whey, or one additional teaspoon of salt

Method for both recipes

Put all the ingredients in a bowl and pound with a wooden pounder, meat hammer, or the pestle from a mortar and pestle until there is lots of juice. Place in a one litre wide mouthed glass or ceramic container, and press down firmly until the juice rises above the cabbage, by about one centimetre. There should be a couple of centimetres of space below the top of the container. Cover and leave at room temperature for three days, then store in the fridge.

Salsa Vegetable Pickle

(no cooking required)

1 kg tomatoes, 1 capsicum, 1 red onion, 4 cloves of garlic, fresh coriander

1-2 teaspoons chillies (optional)

Wash and chop everything up, mix it all together, pack tightly into a jar, leaving a 1cm space at the top. Cover, but don't seal. In a few days bubbles will start to appear. The jar may overflow, so place it on a plate. When the bubbling settles, seal the jar and it's ready to eat.

To stop further fermentation store in the fridge. Start eating small quantities and gradually increase the amount. Eat within two weeks.

APPENDIX D
ALLERGY TESTING

Allergy causes immediate and striking symptoms: redness, swelling of eyes and airways with itching. If severe, an allergic, or anaphylactic reaction can be life-threatening and requires urgent medical care.

Sensitivity causes more subtle, often delayed symptoms, like stomach pain, eczema, headaches and behavioural problems. The challenge with sensitivities, is that because symptoms are delayed and can develop days after exposure, it is difficult to determine precisely which food or foods have caused symptoms.

ALLERGY TESTS

Allergy testing is generally done by a medical practitioner, to find out the severity of allergies, and whether your child needs an *Epipen*[18].

---

[18] Epipen is a medical device for injecting adrenaline with an auto-injector to treat anaphylaxis. It is prescribed by medical doctors following diagnosis of severe allergies.

IgE Food Allergy Panel

An IgE blood test shows the presence of allergies. Further testing is needed to identify specific allergens.

RAST Test (Radioallergosorbent test)

Known allergens are mixed with the patient's serum to see the reaction. This is a 'basic' allergy test, still used by medical practitioners to assess rudimentary allergy status.

Skin Prick Tests

Skin prick testing involves placing a drop of a dilute allergen on the skin which is then pricked. If a red welt develops, the child is considered allergic to that substance. The size of the welt determines how allergic the child is. This test is done by an immunologist which requires a referral from your doctor.

FOOD SENSITIVITY TESTS

IgG and IgA

IgG and IgA tests are both blood tests. Blood can be taken at a laboratory or a finger-prick test can be done at home, using a test kit.

IgG (Immunoglobulin G) and IgA (Immunoglobulin A) are different parts of the immune system from IgE. IgG is the most common test used to assess food sensitivity.

Where there is an inflammatory condition like severe eczema or inflammatory bowel disease (eg Crohn's disease), an IgA food sensitivity panel is also used,

TREATMENT

The key treatment for both IgE mediated allergic responses and IgG or IgA sensitivity reactions is to avoid the offending substance whether it is food or environmental (mould or pollen).

Desensitising

Desensitising protocols, using tiny amounts of the offending foods, can be used effectively to reduce sensitivity and allergy.

Medical desensitisation for severe allergies is conducted under medical supervision and can be effective when there are one or two allergies that need treating. When there is a wide range of food and environmental allergies, wholistic treatment is needed.

Other desensitising methods are:

- Homeopathy
- Kinesiology
- NAET[19].

---

[19] NAET: Nambudripad's Allergy Elimination Technique. See http://www. naet.com for a practitioner in your country and area.

Generalised treatment:

Reducing allergic or hypersensitive responses require ongoing nutritional and immune support from a health professional. Avoiding allergens until a child is more mature is a common approach. Attending to gut health is key. Also attending to nutritional immune factors is important, such as vitamins A, C, D and the mineral zinc.

With time and patience, identifying specific allergens and providing healthcare according to needs, children can grow out of all but the most severe allergies.

APPENDIX E
RESTORING GUT FUNCTION

Poor diet, too many antibiotics and some medications disrupt normal gut function, leading to tummy pain, offensive bowel motions and flatulence. Since 70-80 per cent of immune function stems from a healthy gut, the result of poor intestinal bacteria can result in poor absorption of nutrients, frequent infections, skin problems and behavioural issues. Sadly, this scenario is a common occurrence nowadays and there is a daunting number of over-the-counter products to address gut problems.

Gut problems may not be obvious in your child. Telltale signs are irregular bowel motions, frequent diarrhoea, mushy, offensive or pebbly stools. The child may or may not complain of tummy pain. If your child suffers from eczema, gets frequent infections, has nervous system symptoms like anxiety, behavioural and learning problems and moodiness, these symptoms are what may lead a practitioner to suspect poor gut function. This is called the 'Gut-Brain axis'.

Achieving and maintaining gut health is a long-term project. Simple, cost effective strategies are easier to manage over time, and limit your expectations of a quick fix. While this is not something that parents should tackle alone, it helps to know what you can do to begin the process. Ultimately, professional help will be needed.

The step-by-step strategy below is systematic and designed to help remove the guesswork about what is causing your child's gut problem. This is one time when slow and steady is more likely to lead to success, rather than looking for a magical solution.

REMOVE · NOURISH ·
RESTORE · MAINTAIN

REMOVE

- *Parasites*

Worms and other parasites disrupt the bowel and therefore your child. These are usually effectively treated with an over-the-counter worming product.

- *Yeast*

Yeast overgrowth, most often Candida albicans, must be reduced before gut function can be normalised. Sugar and starchy food must be avoided completely long-term to properly treat yeast overgrowth.

- *Bacteria*

Too much of the wrong bacteria, or too few of some organisms, will disturb gut function.

- *Food Triggers*

Food allergies and sensitivities cause ongoing gut inflammation which will not heal until the offending foods are removed from the diet.

Find out precise food sensitivities, so you can get on the right treatment path sooner rather than later. While most common food sensitivities are gluten, egg and dairy, these may not be a child's only trigger foods.

Tests

Your practitioner may suggest these blood tests for food sensitivity and allergy:

- Coeliac disease
- Food allergy IgE
- Food Sensitivities IgG and IgA. See Appendix D (Allergy Testing).

NOURISH

The more severely the gut is affected, the less able it is to absorb nutrients. Therefore, supplements are a necessary part of the process of gut healing.

Some *nutrients needed for normal gut function:*

- L - Glutamine (this amino acid is a key factor in healing leaky gut).
- Magnesium
- Vitamins A & D
- Zinc.

RESTORE GUT FLORA

Having removed aggravating factors and tended to nutrition, then it is time to recolonise the gut with *beneficial* bacteria to restore proper gut and immune function.

Beneficial bacteria and yeasts are collectively known as probiotics.

Give your child fermented foods daily. Kefir yoghurt — a cheap, homemade superfood containing the widest range of bacteria for just the price of the milk used. See Appendix C.

MAINTAIN

Continue probiotic therapy and healthy diet. Keep a watchful eye for old symptoms reappearing. Behavioural change can be the first sign of gut dysfunction returning.

Find out precise food sensitivities, so you can get on the right treatment path sooner rather than later.

APPENDIX F
IMMUNITY

The rate of childhood allergies is increasing. Health authorities predicted that allergies will affect *50 per cent of populations in developed countries by 2020.* Allergic reactions are a result of disordered immunity which invariably relates to gut health.

Some factors:

Medications

A history of antibiotic and/or paracetamol use since birth or before, into the first two or three years of life is now commonplace. While antibiotics target disease-causing bacteria, they also erode gut bacteria, affecting the 80% of immune function that is generated by a healthy gut. Both of these medicines are known to predispose to allergies.

Diet

Increased sugar and starchy foods in average diets affect gut bacteria by encouraging more yeasts and overgrowth of harmful bacteria.

Nutrients

Many children with immune challenges are deficient in zinc, iron, magnesium, vitamins A and D. These nutrients are essential for healthy immune and gut function.

Alarming Trends

Growing numbers of children with ADD, ADHD, dyslexia, dyspraxia, autism and Asperger's Syndrome is a new phenomenon. These children often have associated immune and gut challenges which may be impacted by the trends mentioned above.

Glyphosate

Traces of this herbicide, can now be found in every part of the world. A huge body of research points to the impact of glyphosate on the gut microbiome, and is therefore impacting on immune systems globally. The only protection against this in your own family is to eat organic, home-grown foods where possible and to filter water.

Key immune-boosting strategies:

- Fermented foods
- Fresh fruit and vegetables
- Eliminate processed foods
- Supplement with zinc
- Ensure adequate iron levels
- Adequate sun exposure without sunscreen for Vitamin D
- Cod Liver Oil and fish oil.

APPENDIX G
OTOVENTS

Ear problems can be made worse when children don't or won't blow their noses properly. *Otovents*, available online, teach children over 3½ years how to blow through their noses, to keep eustachian tubes open and prevent the middle ear from becoming blocked. This really helps some children with frequent ear infections and glue ear.

Using a plastic nose piece with a specially made balloon fitted over it, the child blows up the balloon with his or her nose. If there is a short stab of pain and a 'pop' when blowing up the balloon, it is a good sign that the eustachian tube has opened.

!! *Use Otovents once your child has recovered from their cold or sore ear.* Refrain from using them while your child has current ear pain, an ear infection or a cold.

Use the *Otovents* twice daily for two weeks. Change the balloons every 3 days, or they lose their effectiveness.

You can use *Otovents* on flights to help with the ear pain that children get during take-offs and landings.

Ear Planes, available from pharmacies at airports can also help this problem.

APPENDIX H:
COMMON FOOD SENSITIVITIES

- Gluten
- Dairy and its products
- Eggs
- Yeast

Gluten

Gluten is found in: wheat (bread, cake, biscuits, pasta) rye, barley, oats plus a range of sauces and gravies. Careful label checking is needed.

Gluten-free grains include:

Rice, corn (maize), soya bean, tapioca, chia, buckwheat, millet, amaranth, sorghum, quinoa, arrowroot.

For the best information on gluten free diets, websites about coeliac disease provide detailed dietary information.

Dairy

'Dairy' foods include all animal milks; cow, goat and sheep and their products of cheese, yoghurt, butter and cream.

Some children are able to tolerate goat's milk in preference to cow's milk. Dairy products occur in a range of baked goods, including breads, so label checking is necessary.

Dairy free products include:

Soy milk, rice milk, oat milk, almond milk, coconut cream and coconut milk. Soy cheese is also available.

Eggs

Eggs are found in a wide range of baked goods, including breads — especially 'gluten free' breads, so check labels. 'Egg replacers' are available.

Yeast

Yeast is found in:

Bread, Beer, *Vegemite*, *Bonox*, *Marmite* or similar spreads. Yeast free breads are available in health food stores and some supermarkets.

APPENDIX I
MEDICINE &
SUPPLEMENT SUPPLIES

Local health food stores, pharmacies and supermarkets have a wide range of products and supplements.

Your local natural health practitioner can supply herbal and homeopathic medicines.

Medicines mentioned throughout this book integrative are available via the Internet, through websites like iherb.com.

APPENDIX J
HOMEOPATHIC MEDICINES

THE MEDICINES

Homeopathic medicines are completely safe for young children to use without side effects. They come in liquid or pillules; both have the same effect. Parents generally prefer liquids because they are easier to give to babies and young children.

The name of each medicine is followed by a number, indicating the potency, or strength of the medicine, eg *Arnica 30c*. Tissue Salts mentioned in this book, are in the '6x' potency and are available online, from integrative doctors, natural therapists and pharmacies in most countries.

CHOOSING A MEDICINE

A homeopathic medicine is chosen according to symptoms. The closer the medicine matches the patient's own particular symptoms, the more effective the medicine is.

DOSING

- If using liquid, a single dose is five drops, or about ¼ of a dropper. Drops are best for children under two years old.
- If using pillules, one dose is two pillules, dissolved under the tongue.

Homeopathic medicines are absorbed through the lining of the mouth and not the stomach. Where possible, give the medicine in a clean mouth, at least five minutes away from eating, drinking, or brushing teeth. For babies and very young children, give the dose as you are able, rather waiting for the right moment!

Generally, give the medicine until there is improvement. After you see the symptoms reduce or disappear, reduce the frequency of dose until the symptoms have settled. **Once symptoms have stopped, stop giving medicine.** (In the same way as a painkiller, repeat the dose when the pain returns.)

If the symptoms remain unchanged:

For hourly doses: Change the medicine if no response after four doses.

For two hourly doses: Change after three doses.

For three hourly doses: Change after three doses.

Four doses daily: Change after 24 hours.

Three doses daily: Change after 48 hours if no response.

Twice daily: Change after two to three days if no response.

Once daily: Change or stop one after one week if no response.

One dose every second day. See your homeopath.

If your child is not improving, seek professional help.

CARING FOR HOMEOPATHIC MEDICINES

When kept in a cool dark place away from aromatic substances, homeopathic pillules remain active indefinitely. If liquids turn cloudy, they need to be replaced.

Liquids are easier and safer to give to babies and children under two years old. Sucking the dropper may introduce bacteria into the bottle. Therefore, put the drops onto a teaspoon and give to your child, or put drops into a little water in a glass.

FINDING A HOMEOPATH

The International Council of Homeopaths website http://www.homeopathy-ich.org lists member countries, their associations and qualified practitioners.

Where to Buy Homeopathic Medicines

Homeopathic medicines are available online, from homeopathic practitioners and some pharmacies, depending on your country.

Australia
Martin & Pleasance www.martinandpleasance.com
Brauer Natural Medicine www.brauer.com.au

Europe - See 'International' below

Indonesia
Tirta Usada, Ubud, Bali
Phone +62 851 001 37375 / +62 812 467 95679

New Zealand
Simillimum Health and Homeopathy
https://www.simillimum.co.nz/index.php/sales

South America - See 'International' below

UK
Ainsworths www.ainsworths.com
Nelson's Homeopathic Pharmacy www.nelsonspharmacy.com
Helios Homeopathy www.helios.co.uk

USA & Canada - See 'International' below

International
Whole Health Now Suppliers and Pharmacies
www.wholehealthnow.com/homeopathy_info/weblinks3.
html

SELECTED BIBLIOGRAPHY

- Encyclopaedia of Food Science & Food Technology & Nutrition 5 ISBN: 0-12-226855-5, ACADEMIC PRESS -> Food Technology and Nutrition.
- Berkow, et al, The Merck Manual, 17th ed, Merck & Co, NJ,
- Boericke, W, Pocket Manual of Homeopathic Materia Medica 9th ed, 1927, B Jain, New Delhi
- Boiron, M & Payre-Ficot, A, Everyday Homeopathy for Pharmacists, Editions Boiron, France, 2000
- Campbell-McBride, N, Gut and Psychology Syndrome, Medinform Publishing, Cambridge, UK, 2004
- Clarke, J, Dictionary of Practical Materia Medica, London, (1900), B Jain, New Delhi
- Fallon, S, Nourishing Traditions, New Trends Publishing, 2001
- Fisher, C, Diseases of Children, B Jain Publishers, New Delhi (1997 reprint)
- Gamble, J, Mastering Homeopathy: Accurate Daily Prescribing for a Successful Practice, Karuna Publishing, Wollongong, 2004
- Handbook of the Tissue Salts, Martin & Pleasance, Melbourne, 1991

- Lockie, A, Family Guide to Homeopathy, The, Hamish Hamilton, London, 1990
- Mathur, K, Principles of Prescribing, B Jain Publishers, New Delhi, 1975
- Osiecki, H, Physicians Handbook of Clinical Nutrition, 6th ed, Bioconcepts Publishing, Brisbane, 2001
- Root-Bernstein, R & M, Honey, Mud & Maggots and Other Medical Marvels, Pan Books, London, 2000
- Tkac, D (Ed), Doctor's Book of Home Remedies, The, Bantam, New York, 1991
- Vermeulen, F, Synoptic Materia Medica, Vols 1 & 2, Merlijn Publishers, The Netherlands, 6th & 2nd eds (2000 & 1998)

WEBSITES

Raising Children Network https://raisingchildren.net.au

The Aurum Project - aurumproject.org.au

Mindd Foundation - https://mindd.org

Karuna Health Care - www.karunahealthcare.com.au

STUDIES

- Neustaedter *Effective Healthcare. The Treatment of persistent glue ear in children.* November 1992 No. 4
- Moskovitz R. *Childhood ear infections: a homeopathic model for diagnosis, treatment and research* Journal American Institute of Homoeopathy Autumn 1994;87: 137-143.
- Neustaedter R. *Management of otitis media with effusion in homoeopathy practice.* Journal American Institute of Homoeopathy 1986;79:133-140.
- De Lange de Klerk ESM, Blommers J, Kuik D J, Bezemer P D, Feenstra L. *Effect of homeopathic medicines on daily burden of symptoms in children with recurrent upper respiratory tract infections.* BMJ 1994: 309: 1329-1372.
- Friese K H. Kruse S. Ludtke R. Moeller H. *The homeopathic treatment of otitis media in children-comparisons with conventional therapy.* I International Journal of Clinical Pharmacology & Therapeutics 1997: 35: 296-301.